MONUMENTAL MILESTONES
GREAT EVENTS OF MODERN TIMES

The Cuban Missile Crisis: The Cold War Goes Hot

Soviet premier Nikita Khrushchev (left), U.S. president John F. Kennedy (center), and Cuban dictator Fidel Castro were the three main figures in the Cuban Missile Crisis.

Mitchell Lane
PUBLISHERS

P.O. Box 196
Hockessin, Delaware 19707

Titles in the Series

MONUMENTAL MILESTONES
GREAT EVENTS OF MODERN TIMES

The Cuban Missile Crisis:
The Cold War Goes Hot

Soviet premier Nikita Khrushchev (left), U.S. president John F. Kennedy (center), and Cuban dictator Fidel Castro were the three main figures in the Cuban Missile Crisis.

Jim Whiting

Mitchell Lane PUBLISHERS

Printing   2   3   4   5   6   7   8

Library of Congress Cataloging-in-Publication Data
   Whiting, Jim, 1943–
     The Cuban Missile Crisis: the Cold War goes hot / by Jim Whiting.
   Includes bibliographical references and index.
   ISBN 1-58415-404-7 (library bound)
   1. Cuban Missile Crisis, 1962—Juvenile literature. I. Title. II. Series.
E841.W495 2005
973.922—dc22
2005009689

ISBN-10: 1-58415-404-7   ISBN-13: 9781584154044

ABOUT THE AUTHOR: Jim Whiting has been a journalist, writer, editor, and photographer for more than 20 years. In addition to a lengthy stint as publisher of *Northwest Runner* magazine, Mr. Whiting has contributed articles to the *Seattle Times*, *Conde Nast Traveler*, *Newsday*, and *Saturday Evening Post*. He has written numerous books for Mitchell Lane in a variety of series. He has also edited more than 100 Mitchell Lane titles. A great lover of classical music and history of modern times, he has written many books for young adults, including *The Life and Times of Irving Berlin* and *The Story of the Attack on Pearl Harbor* (Mitchell Lane). He lives in Washington state with his wife and two teenage sons.

PHOTO CREDITS: Cover, pp. 1, 3—Cecil Stoughton/Time Life Pictures/Getty Images and Library of Congress; p. 6—Allan Jackson/Hulton Archive/Getty Images; pp. 8, 12, 22, 25, 28—Library of Congress; p. 18—NSArchive; pp. 20, 30, 38—Air Force Archives.

PUBLISHER'S NOTE: This story is based on the author's extensive research, which he believes to be accurate. Documentation of such research is contained on page 47.

The internet sites referenced herein were active as of the publication date. Due to the fleeting nature of some web sites, we cannot guarantee they will all be active when you are reading this book.

MONUMENTAL MILESTONES
GREAT EVENTS OF MODERN TIMES

Contents
The Cuban Missile Crisis
Jim Whiting

*For Your Information

Members of the U.S. 1st Army shake hands with Soviet troops on the banks of Germany's Elbe River on April 25, 1945.

From left, the American soldiers are PFC John A. Metzger, Delbert E. Philpott and Pvt. Thomas B. Summers. The event united the two principal Allies who had brought about the defeat of Nazi Germany in World War II. Within two weeks the war in Europe had ended.

The Roots of a Conflict

One of the most famous photographs of World War II was taken late in April 1945. It showed jubilant soldiers from the United States and the Soviet Union as they met near Germany's Elbe River. The photo seemed to symbolize the alliance between the two nations that had defeated German dictator Adolf Hitler and ended the threat of Nazi tyranny.

It was a very uneasy alliance. The U.S. and Soviet governments deeply distrusted each other. This mutual distrust went back more than a quarter of a century. In 1917, a year before the end of World War I, the Communists took over the government of Russia. Nicholas II, the last of the czars who had ruled Russia for centuries, was imprisoned and later executed. In 1922, Russia became the largest and most important member of the Soviet Union. The new nation's leaders believed in eliminating private property and having the government control the economy. These principles were the opposite of the capitalist economic systems that existed in the United States, Great Britain, and other Western nations. As a result, a small contingent of American troops that had been fighting in World War I landed in Russia. They were accompanied by a larger force of soldiers from other Western powers, and their mission was to overthrow the new Communist government. The attempt failed, and the Americans suffered more than 400 casualties.

The United States and the Soviet Union broke off official diplomatic relations. That means they did not exchange ambassadors. By 1933, however, both began to feel threatened by a new danger that was surfacing. It was Germany, which had been crushed at the end of World War I. Under the leadership of its Nazi dictator Adolf Hitler, Germany began an aggressive program of military expansion that led to the outbreak of World War II in 1939.

Less than two years later, the German army invaded the Soviet Union and slashed deep into Soviet territory. U.S. president Franklin D. Roosevelt and British prime minister Winston Churchill decided to help Soviet dictator Joseph Stalin. If the Germans defeated the Soviets, many German soldiers would be freed up to attack Britain. If Britain fell, all of Europe could fall under Nazi domination—which in turn could place the United States in danger. However, not even the common goal of defeating Hitler could eliminate the deep mistrust between the United States and Russia. They withheld a great deal of information from each other—including their plans for what would happen after the war.

Soviet dictator Joseph Stalin (left) and U.S. president Franklin D. Roosevelt.

The two leaders, along with British prime minister Winston Churchill, met in February 1945 in the Soviet city of Yalta to plan for the end of World War II and its aftermath.

1

When it surrendered in May 1945, Germany was divided between the United States, Great Britain, France, and the Soviet Union. A similar division occurred in Germany's capital city of Berlin, which was located far inside the Soviet sector. It became apparent that the four powers had major differences. The United States, Great Britain, and France wanted democratic elections. The Soviets had no intention of allowing that to happen.

These differences led to what became known as the Cold War, which soon spread beyond Germany to encompass the entire world. Rather than open conflict, this new style of warfare was characterized by an increasingly dangerous arms race, extensive spy networks, military alliances, attempts to influence or control the governments of as many other nations as possible, trade agreements, and more.

Propaganda—the war of words—was also important. Just over a year after World War II ended, Churchill made a famous speech called "The Sinews of Peace." In it, he said: "From Stettin in the Baltic to Trieste in the Adriatic, an iron curtain has descended across the Continent. Behind that line lie all the capitals of the ancient states of Central and Eastern Europe. Warsaw, Berlin, Prague, Vienna, Budapest, Belgrade, Bucharest and Sofia, all these famous cities and the populations around them lie in what I must call the Soviet sphere, and all are subject, in one form or another, not only to Soviet influence but to a very high and, in many cases, increasing measure of control from Moscow [the capital of the Soviet Union]."[1]

For many years, the phrase "behind the iron curtain" referred to the Soviet Union and the countries in Eastern Europe that it controlled. It implied that the people living there were victims of tyranny. Liberating them became an important goal of the countries in the West.

The situation came to a head in June 1948. The Soviets blockaded all roads leading to Berlin. The United States led a massive airlift that flew in thousands of tons of relief supplies every day. Nearly eleven months later, the Soviets opened up the roads again. It was the first time that Berlin had become a flash point in the Cold War. It wouldn't be the last.

By that time the United States, Great Britain, and ten other nations had formed the North Atlantic Treaty Organization (NATO). The members pledged that they would regard an attack on any member as an attack on all of them. They all believed that the source of such an attack would be the Soviet Union.

A few months later, the United States received a severe shock. The Soviet Union had successfully tested an atomic bomb. That ended the U.S. monopoly on atomic weapons and served to intensify the Cold War. A few years later the rivalry became even more intense when both sides developed far more powerful hydrogen bombs. They now had the ability to inflict catastrophic losses on each other.

The stakes were raised in 1955 when the Soviet Union and the Eastern European nations under Communist rule formed the Warsaw Pact. Similar to NATO, the Warsaw Pact was a pledge among member nations to protect one another. NATO and the Warsaw Pact nations conducted many large-scale military exercises, believing that war between the two sides would break out, most likely in Europe. Both world wars had started in Europe. With hundreds of thousands of armed men within a relatively short distance of each other, there were many scenarios of a possible World War III originating there as well.

But when the world came perilously close to plunging into another horrible war—a war in which the use of nuclear weapons could have made it the most destructive in human history—the site wasn't Europe at all. It was a very unlikely place, thousands of miles away on the sun-splashed shores of a Caribbean nation.

The site was Cuba.

One of the most important examples of the wartime mistrust between the Soviet Union and the United States was the Manhattan Project, the super-secret and very expensive undertaking by the United States to develop an atomic bomb. American authorities didn't say anything to the Soviets about the project. Yet the Soviets were well aware of what was going on, because some of the scientists involved in the Manhattan Project were passing along the results of their work.

Two of the most important spies were Klaus Fuchs and Ted Hall. Born in 1911, Fuchs was a member of the Communist Party in Germany. He fled the Nazis in the mid-1930s and moved to England to avoid being arrested. Soon he was working for the British on their atomic program. He came to the United States in 1943 to work on the Manhattan Project, where he was one of the most important scientists.

Hall was a brilliant young American physicist who skipped several grades while he was growing up; he graduated from Harvard in 1944 with a degree in physics. He was only eighteen. He was quickly hired to work on the Manhattan Project and began spying for the Soviets soon afterward.

It is estimated that the secrets passed to the Soviets by Fuchs, Hall, and others helped the Soviets to develop their own nuclear weapons between two and eight years earlier than they otherwise would have.

Ethel and Julius Rosenberg

It wasn't until 1949 that the existence of the spy ring was finally proven. By then, Fuchs was living in England. He was sentenced to fourteen years in prison, the maximum allowable under English law. After serving nine years, he was released and moved to Communist East Germany, where he lived for the rest of his life. Americans Julius and Ethel Rosenberg were executed in 1953 for their role in passing the atomic secrets to the Soviets. Two other men who were also involved received prison terms rather than the death penalty because they cooperated with the investigation. Incredibly, Ted Hall was never arrested.

Cuban dictator Fidel Castro hugs Soviet leader Nikita Khrushchev.

To the leaders of Democratic governments, photos such as this one symbolized the close alliance between the two Communist countries. They became increasingly concerned about the presence of a Communist government less than 100 miles from U.S. soil.

Unmasking a Deception

For nearly four centuries following its discovery by Christopher Columbus in 1492, Cuba remained under Spanish rule. It wasn't until 1902, three years after the U.S. victory in the Spanish-American War, that Cuba became an independent nation. Because it was only ninety miles from the southern tip of Florida, the island was heavily influenced by the United States. A number of U.S. companies set up profitable operations there.

Starting in the mid-1930s, Cuban politics were dominated by Fulgencio Batista, who ruled as dictator until 1940 and then as president until 1944. After a few years of retirement and a military coup, he was returned to power in 1952. He ruled primarily to benefit himself and a handful of friends. Many Cubans lived in poverty.

Almost immediately after returning to power, Batista was opposed by a young lawyer named Fidel Castro. After an unsuccessful attack on an army barracks in 1953, Castro was arrested and sentenced to fifteen years in prison. He was released a year later when Batista pardoned all Cuban political prisoners. Castro went to Mexico to continue the revolution.

On Christmas Day, 1956, Castro snuck back into Cuba, heading a small band of followers that included his brother Raul. They hid in the rugged Sierra Maestra Mountains in the southeast corner of Cuba and began a series of hit-and-run attacks. Even though Batista's army was many times the size of Castro's and far better equipped, they could not defeat the rebels (although they continually claimed that they had). Castro benefited from the lack of trust and loyalty that most Cubans felt toward Batista. He also benefited from the force of his personality. He was a dynamic leader who made it clear that he wanted to help Cuba's people raise their standard of living. Gradually Castro's forces increased in size and pushed westward toward the country's capital city of Havana. In the early morning darkness of New Year's Day, 1959, Batista fled. Castro arrived in Havana to a tumultuous welcome. He was just thirty-two years old.

Soon afterward, Castro came to the United States for a tour. For the most part, he received an enthusiastic reception. His schedule included a visit to Harvard University. He told McGeorge Bundy, one of the school's most important professors, that he had applied for admission to Harvard Law School in 1948 but had been turned down. Bundy, impressed with his guest, said that he was welcome to attend now. A few years later Bundy would be making arrangements of a very different nature for Castro.

After some initial hesitation, the U.S. government extended diplomatic recognition to Castro. The relationship quickly soured. The Cuban government either took over American-owned businesses in Cuba or placed severe restrictions on them. Suspicions that Castro was a Communist grew when he appealed to the Soviet Union for help. Soviet leaders concluded an agreement to exchange Soviet oil for Cuban sugar. That was followed by loans and additional assistance.

On January 3, 1961, President Dwight D. Eisenhower broke off diplomatic relations with Cuba. He was convinced that Castro was a Communist—and a Communist who wanted other countries to adopt the same form of government.

Eisenhower and other U.S. officials were afraid that Cuba's example could spread to other nations in the Caribbean and in Central and South America. They didn't want any of these countries to adopt Communist governments. It was bad enough that such a charismatic figure as Fidel Castro was less than a hundred miles from Florida. They believed that the situation would become more dangerous if Castro were to have allies close by.

Even before breaking off diplomatic relations, Eisenhower had ordered the Central Intelligence Agency (CIA) to begin planning for Castro's overthrow by anti-Castro rebels. When Castro came to power or soon afterward, thousands of Cubans fled the country and settled in south Florida. Many of them had been members of the Cuban army before their departure. At first the plan consisted of guerrilla operations, similar to the ones that Castro had employed following his return from Mexico. Gradually it broadened to include an invasion. Enough men would land to establish a beachhead. This beachhead, it was believed, would incite Castro's opponents inside Cuba to join the revolt against him. As the revolt gained momentum, the United States would become involved. But in the beginning, it was important to make the attack appear to be entirely the work of the exiles.

After narrowly defeating Vice President Richard M. Nixon in the elections held the previous November, incoming president John F. Kennedy learned of the invasion plans. At first he was hesitant to adopt them. Assurances from his top advisers convinced him that the invasion would easily succeed. They were confident that the Cuban people would rise up against Castro. Kennedy ordered the CIA to continue with its planning and training.

The invasion, which became known as the Bay of Pigs after the name of the landing site on Cuba's southern coast, began on April 15, 1961. Nothing went right. Nearly all the invaders were killed or captured. The attack was crushed within three days. Its legacy would linger much longer.

The ill-fated invasion served to cement Castro's power and prestige in Cuba. In the eyes of the Cuban people, Castro had taken on the mighty United States and won. It was an enormous embarrassment for Kennedy, who had refused to allow American Marines and aircraft to become involved. The Cubans became even closer to their Soviet allies.

Two months later, Kennedy and Soviet premier Nikita S. Khrushchev met at a summit conference in Vienna, Austria. Most of their conversations revolved around mutual disarmament and the status of Berlin. Cuba was barely mentioned. The conference didn't solve any of the problems between the two superpowers. However, it did give Khrushchev the impression that the new American president wasn't very tough. Khrushchev, who had had to be very tough to survive and thrive in the Communist Party, wasn't impressed.

Six months later, Castro gave a famous speech in which he declared that he was a Communist and had always been a Communist. At the urging of U.S. secretary of state Dean Rusk, the Organization of American States (OAS) voted to expel Cuba in January 1962. Rusk also convinced more than a dozen members to break diplomatic relations with Cuba. In February, Kennedy cut off virtually all trade with the island nation. It was a significant economic blow. Castro blamed what he called "Yankee imperialism" for these actions. He remained defiant.

The CIA continued its efforts to undermine him. By then, these efforts had become known as Operation Mongoose. The plans consisted of several options for getting rid of Castro. Mongoose was a secret—to Americans. Without much difficulty, some members of Castro's intelligence service had infiltrated the group. Coupled with well-publicized American military exercises in the Caribbean that were plainly directed against him—one even carried the code name of Operation Ortsac, or "Castro" spelled backward—it was obvious to Castro and to Khrushchev that the United States was still determined to overthrow the Cuban government.

Cuba wasn't the only source of concern for Khrushchev. Even though the Soviets had stunned the United States in 1957 by launching *Sputnik I*, the world's first artificial satellite, it seemed apparent to him that the Soviets had fallen significantly behind both in the number of nuclear warheads that the two countries controlled and the delivery systems for these warheads. Khrushchev even believed that the United States was considering a first strike against his country to take advantage of this superiority. The government of East Germany had erected a wall dividing Berlin in the summer of 1961, so tensions there were still at a high point.

It is likely that Khrushchev thought of the solution to his concerns sometime in April 1962. He would install Soviet ballistic guided missiles in Cuba. These missiles were capable of delivering nuclear warheads over long distances. He believed that he could conceal the operation long enough to allow the missiles to become fully operational. He also believed that once that happened, the weak Kennedy would not do anything about it. Besides, he reasoned, similar American missiles, pointing at the Soviet Union, had already been installed in Turkey. He was only doing what the Americans had already done.

Khrushchev may also have believed that the United States didn't have enough respect for him or for his country. Making such a bold move would make Kennedy aware of how powerful the Soviet Union really was. It would also provide a dramatic reassurance to Castro that Khrushchev was solidly behind him.

In May, Khrushchev proposed the idea to other Soviet leaders. Even though it was a radical idea—the Soviets had never installed nuclear missiles outside their borders—they agreed with Khrushchev. In July, Castro's trusted brother Raul went to Moscow for a series of meetings. During this time, he reached agreement with the Soviets to supply Cuba with a variety of weapons. These included defensive equipment such as tanks and surface-to-air missiles (SAMs). They also included the ballistic missiles.

The Soviets began a massive sealift to transport all this equipment. Starting in late July, nearly a hundred large cargo ships left the Soviet Union for Cuba. The Soviets attempted to disguise what they were doing. Thousands of military personnel arrived in cruise ships. As soon as they got off, they lined up in perfect order on the dock—something that cruise ship passengers would never do. To preserve secrecy, these

A photo of a missile site in Cuba taken by a U.S. U-2 spy plane.

Photos such as this one revealed the existence of Medium-Range Ballistic Missiles (MRBMs) in Cuba. These weapons could deliver a nuclear warhead to many U.S. cities.

personnel were not told where they were going before their departure. Many had brought winter clothing and skis.

"If we'd known that, it would *really* have upset us," Robert McNamara, who was Kennedy's defense secretary, joked many years later. "We would have thought they were planning to invade Vermont."[1]

There was no joking at the time, as it soon became apparent in the United States that a major military buildup was taking place. Spies and Cubans fleeing to Florida brought word of huge construction projects. In August, CIA photo analysts discovered the existence of several sites containing surface-to-air missiles. Khrushchev continually insisted that everything arriving in Cuba was defensive in nature. President Kennedy and his advisers were willing to believe him. They agreed that the Cubans had a right to defend themselves.

The increasing Soviet presence in Cuba became an issue in the upcoming U.S. Congressional elections. Republicans used the buildup as a campaign issue, criticizing Kennedy for allowing it to happen. Public opinion polls showed a decline in voter approval of Kennedy's handling of the situation. On September 4, he issued a public warning to the Soviet Union and Cuba against bringing in any offensive weapons. While it wasn't immediately apparent, Kennedy had drawn a line in the sand. He would tolerate defensive military equipment. He would not tolerate anything else—especially missiles with nuclear warheads.

The next few weeks saw a steady stream of messages from the Soviet Union containing assurances that the buildup remained defensive in nature. One of these was a letter to Kennedy. Khrushchev had personally signed it. He assured Kennedy that he had no intention of locating offensive missiles outside his country's borders.

As the buildup continued, the photo analysts were working overtime. Their boss, CIA director John McCone, was becoming especially alarmed. He wondered why the SAM sites were being constructed. He thought they might have some other purpose than general island defense. He reasoned that they were there to protect something specific. Something like nuclear missiles. Hardly anyone agreed with him.

Early in October, Kennedy authorized a series of overflights by U-2 spy planes. The U-2 was a specially designed airplane that could soar to heights of more than thirteen miles above the earth. It was fitted with cameras so finely tuned that they could pick up golf balls lying on the ground. Cloudy weather postponed the flights for several days.

On October 14, 1962, the weather improved enough for a U-2 to take off. Its assignment was to photograph the area around San Cristóbal in western Cuba. The pilot took several thousand photos. When he landed, the film was rushed to the National Photographic Intelligence Center (NPIC) near Washington, D.C.

The following day, NPIC specialists began poring over the photos. They quickly recognized the telltale shape of a SAM installation. But the site contained several large objects that at first couldn't be identified. More experts were brought in. Soon they realized that they were looking at something far more dangerous than SAMs. They saw the shape of SS-4 Medium-Range Ballistic Missiles (MRBMs). With a range of more than a thousand miles, they brought most of the United States east of the Mississippi well within reach of their nuclear warheads.

That evening, NPIC director Arthur Lundahl picked up the telephone. He began making calls to important government officials.

One of the first officials on Lundahl's list was McGeorge Bundy. Now Kennedy's national security adviser, he was the former Harvard professor who had invited Castro to attend law school there. Bundy decided not to inform the president that night. Kennedy had just returned from several days of intensive campaigning. He was exhausted. Bundy wanted him to get a good night's sleep. He believed that restful nights in the upcoming days would be rare. He was correct.

A modern-day photo of a U-2 spy plane.

The exceptionally wide wings and lightweight construction allowed the U-2 to fly much higher than other aircraft. Its missions during the Cold War brought back a great deal of useful information.

President Kennedy and his brother Robert were deeply humiliated by the failure of the Bay of Pigs invasion. Getting rid of Castro became almost an obsession with them. In November 1961, they directed the CIA to establish a secret program that would eliminate Castro, either by fomenting a rebellion inside Cuba through acts of sabotage or by assassinating the Cuban leader or tarnishing his heroic image among his people. The program was named Operation Mongoose, and its headquarters were in Miami.

In spite of the efforts of several hundred CIA operatives and thousands of Cuban exiles—as well as meetings between CIA officials and the Mafia to get practical advice on killing Castro—Operation Mongoose had little effect. While Castro would later complain of more than twenty attempts by the CIA to kill him, none came close to success. When the missile crisis ended, so did Operation Mongoose. A year and a half later, President Lyndon Johnson ordered an end to all efforts to assassinate Castro.

Fidel Castro (center)

Some of the plots against Castro cooked up during Operation Mongoose seem very bizarre. They included the following:

- Putting an untraceable poison into Castro's favorite brand of cigars.
- Booby-trapping attractive seashells and planting them on the seabed in areas where Castro, who enjoyed scuba diving, would be sure to see them; they would explode if he picked them up.
- Devising a special wet suit that would be heavily laden with infectious germs.
- Spraying a television studio with a hallucinogenic drug just before Castro gave a speech so that he would babble like an idiot.
- Dousing his shoes with a drug that would cause his beard—perhaps his most distinctive feature—to fall out and thereby make him appear less formidable.
- Distributing a fake photo showing a very overweight Castro with two lovely women. They stood in a room with very elegant furnishings. Just behind them was a table brimming with food. At that time, most Cubans weren't getting enough to eat. The photo implied that Castro was living much better than his people.

President John F. Kennedy (left) and his brother, Attorney General Robert Kennedy.

The President had a great deal of trust and confidence in his brother. He often sought advice from Robert.

ExComm

Just before nine o'clock on the morning of October 16, Bundy broke the news to the president. Kennedy was still in his pajamas, reading the morning newspapers. While Kennedy was furious with Khrushchev for lying to him, he knew that he needed to keep the explosive information as secret as possible until he had decided how to respond.

He immediately contacted his most trusted advisers, asking them to come to the White House as quickly and as quietly as possible. Aware of the historical nature of what was about to begin, Kennedy secretly taped all the conversations. The group soon became known as the Executive Committee of the National Security Council, or ExComm for short. Though the makeup of the group underwent some changes during the course of the crisis, the most important members included

- Attorney General Robert Kennedy, the president's brother and closest adviser
- McGeorge Bundy, National Security Adviser
- Charles Bohlen, former ambassador to the Soviet Union
- Dean Rusk, Secretary of State
- George Ball, Undersecretary of State
- Edwin M. Martin, Assistant Secretary of State for Latin America
- Llewellyn Thompson, Ambassador at Large
- Adlai Stevenson, U.S. Ambassador to the UN
- Robert McNamara, Secretary of Defense
- Roswell Gilpatric, Deputy Secretary of Defense

- Paul Nitze, Assistant Secretary of Defense
- General Maxwell Taylor, Chairman of the Joint Chiefs of Staff
- John McCone, Director of the CIA
- C. Douglas Dillon, Treasury Secretary
- Theodore Sorenson, speechwriter and special counsel for the president

As several participants later commented, assembling ExComm was an unusual way of dealing with a crisis. Some of the members with traditional backgrounds in government were upset. They didn't like the committee's relatively unstructured nature. Kennedy made it clear that he chose this arrangement so that the men could speak their minds freely. Sometimes he would even leave the room so that his presence wouldn't influence the discussions. But he also made it clear that the ultimate decision lay with him.

The men were baffled as to why Khrushchev had taken this dangerous step, and they proposed several possible explanations. It seemed apparent to them that Khrushchev believed he could push Kennedy around. It seemed equally obvious that anything less than firm, immediate action would only encourage Khrushchev to begin throwing his weight around in other political hot spots, such as Berlin.

The group considered its non-military options. One was to simply do nothing. Another was to seek a diplomatic solution. It didn't take long to reject these. One reason was the election season. Kennedy couldn't appear to be soft on Communism or his party would suffer a disastrous defeat at the polls.

Consequently, ExComm decided that a military solution was necessary. The committee identified four options. One was a surgical strike, an air raid that would target only the known offensive missile sites. Second was a broader air strike that would include fighter bases and SAM sites. Both types of air attacks would be launched without warning. Third was a ground invasion involving thousands of U.S. troops. Fourth was a naval blockade of Cuba. While a blockade would have no effect on material already there, it would prevent further missiles and warheads from arriving.

ExComm split into two groups. One favored direct military action, either an air strike or an invasion. They wanted the strongest possible response and didn't believe that Khrushchev would parry with nuclear weapons. They argued that Khrushchev simply didn't care strongly enough about Castro to risk all-out war. The other group advocated a blockade as a milder response. They noted that Khrushchev was notoriously unpredictable. He could well order the use of nuclear weapons in response to a U.S. attack.

The blockade advocates had another point. It had been just over twenty years since the Japanese attack on Pearl Harbor had catapulted the United States into World War II. The attack had enraged the American people, causing them to unite in a fierce determination to crush the Japanese. President Kennedy and several ExComm members had fought in the conflict, so it was on their minds.

Robert Kennedy said, "I can't see letting my brother be a Tōjō [the military leader of Japan in World War II] and make an unannounced attack on a little country . . . all our heritage and our ideals would be repugnant to such a sneak military attack."[1]

Perhaps the most powerful reason was that if a blockade were tried and failed, the air strike and other military options would still be on the table. While the element of total surprise would have been lost, partial tactical surprise could still be achieved.

The group couldn't come to a consensus. The president ordered them to return and continue the discussions.

The need for secrecy created some unusual arrangements. The ExComm members knew that it would seem strange if they all began canceling some of their normal appointments. As a result, they met at times—often late at night—that didn't conflict with their normal daily schedules. There was another problem. So many limousines simultaneously arriving at the White House would arouse curiosity. Most of the ExComm members were driven to the nearby Treasury Department instead. The building was connected to the White House by a private underground passage.

It was hardest on the president. Kennedy's schedule was so well publicized that any changes would have raised eyebrows and invited unwanted questions. He also had to be an excellent actor. Soon after receiving word of the existence of the missiles, he had to meet and greet several astronauts and their families. He even took the children outside to see his daughter's pony. No one suspected that anything was wrong.

The following day—October 17—Kennedy's schedule called for him to make a campaign stop in Connecticut. When he returned, Kennedy learned that a few people were starting to become suspicious, despite the precautions that were being taken. Reaching a conclusion became even more pressing.

On Thursday, October 18, Kennedy had a previously scheduled meeting with Soviet foreign minister Andrei Gromyko. Gromyko reiterated his government's position that all the weapons in Cuba were defensive. Kennedy, with the photos that proved Gromyko was lying stashed in a desk drawer a few feet away, simply repeated the U.S. position that offensive weapons were unacceptable.

By then Kennedy was aware of an even graver danger. Additional U-2 photos revealed the existence of SS-5 missiles. These were Intermediate-Range Ballistic Missiles (IRBMs) with nearly double the range of the MRBMs. They not only brought many more American cities within reach, but they could also strike U.S. long-range missiles in the Midwest.

General Taylor, who had previously urged Kennedy to consider a massive air strike, changed his mind. He decided an invasion was the only realistic possibility for removing the missiles.

That night, elegantly attired guests arrived at the State Department building for a dinner honoring Gromyko. The ceremony was held on the building's eighth floor. One floor below, ExComm was holding another secret session.

The president met with the Joint Chiefs of Staff the following morning, then left for a campaign swing through the Midwest. He wasn't completely satisfied with the ExComm deliberations. He ordered each group to submit a written proposal to the other side, which would then criticize the position.

The time for talking was coming to an end. Kennedy knew that he would soon have to make his decision. Reporters familiar with the Washington scene sensed that something big was happening under their noses. Kennedy knew they would soon begin asking awkward questions.

While he was in Chicago, President Kennedy got a phone call from his brother, telling him that ExComm was still divided. Robert urged the president to return to Washington immediately, even though his campaign trip was scheduled to run for a few days longer. To explain his sudden departure, the president asked press secretary Pierre Salinger to announce that he had a cold. Salinger—who knew nothing of ExComm—was incredulous. Kennedy appeared to be in robust health.

President Kennedy went to the White House swimming pool as soon as he returned on Saturday. When he emerged, Robert Kennedy was waiting for him, and the two men headed for what would prove to be the decisive ExComm meeting. The president polled the members individually, then made his momentous decision.

The United States would respond with a blockade.

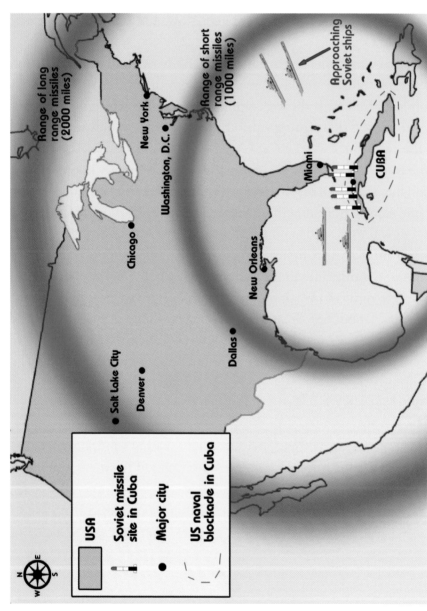

This map illustrates why the existence of offensive missiles in Cuba was such a threat. The weapons were within range of many American cities. Soviet ships carrying even more missiles were heading toward Cuba. If they had been installed, even more American cities could have become targets.

Before the era of spy satellites, the United States needed a way to fly inside the Soviet Union and take aerial photographs. They needed to get a good idea of Soviet missile and bomber capabilities. The U-2 spy plane was developed for that purpose. Using funds authorized by President Dwight D. Eisenhower, the Lockheed Corporation designed and built the first U-2 in a period of less than a year. Similar to a glider, the airplane was designed to be as simple and as lightweight as possible. It was fifty feet long with a wingspan of eighty feet; it made its first operational flight in 1956. With a ceiling of 70,000 feet, the U-2 could fly nearly four miles higher than any Soviet fighter aircraft. It had a range of 3,000 miles and a maximum speed of about 450 miles per hour.

The U-2 made numerous flights over the Soviet Union without a hitch for four years. However, everything changed on May 1, 1960, when a U-2 piloted by Francis Gary Powers was shot down. The incident created a great deal of embarrassment for the United States, and caused a summit conference between President Eisenhower and Soviet premier Nikita Khrushchev to be canceled. Powers was sentenced to ten years in a Soviet prison for espionage, but was released within two years in exchange for a Soviet spy.

While the Powers incident marked the end of U-2 overflights of the Soviet Union, the airplane continued to serve a vital role in other areas of the world. Eventually spy satellites replaced it for espionage, but it has been used for other operations. Some U-2s, the U-2Rs, are a larger version of the original aircraft. They have performed military missions such as helping to determine the location of Iraqi Scud missile launchers during the 1991 Gulf War. Others have conducted high-altitude research.

U-2R

A U.S. Air Force B-52 heavy bomber drops a load of bombs on a target. Even though they are more than 40 years old, dozens of U.S. Air Force B-52 bombers are still in active service.

The B-52 bombers carry up to 35 tons of weapons. These range from conventional bombs to cruise missiles. Eight jet engines power the planes at speeds up to 650 miles per hour at altitudes as high as 50,000 feet.

To the Brink

With the decision made, many things had to be done. The armed forces had already been put on alert. Thousands of troops were on their way to Florida. Dozens of Navy ships received orders to sail, sometimes so hurriedly that they had to leave part of their crews behind. Air Force jets began flying in to bases from which they could more easily reach Cuba. Eight-engined B-52 bombers with nuclear weapons were kept aloft at all times. Some were only a few minutes' flying time from their targets in the Soviet Union.

One small change had to be made. The word "blockade" legally referred to a state of war existing between two countries. Since the United States and the Soviet Union were not at war, the upcoming action was referred to as a "quarantine."

On Sunday morning, still unsure if he had made the right decision, Kennedy met with Tactical Air Force commander Walter Sweeney. Kennedy asked Sweeney if he was confident that he could destroy all the Soviet offensive missiles. Sweeney answered honestly that he could get most but not guarantee complete destruction. A few could survive to strike American cities. That helped to reassure Kennedy.

With the capital buzzing that something was afoot, Kennedy ordered a variety of government officials to come in their limousines to the west gate of the White House. Reporters knew that something was brewing, but the sheer number of arrivals kept them from an accurate assessment of the situation. In the meantime, ExComm members used the now-familiar Treasury Department route for a midafternoon meeting.

Some newspapers, such as the *New York Times* and *Washington Post,* appeared to be very close to understanding what was going on. Kennedy personally spoke with their publishers and asked them not to print everything they knew. They agreed.

Monday was an especially busy day. ExComm officials consulted with congressional leaders. A few did not support the quarantine. They believed that sooner or later the United States would have to invade Cuba, and that doing it sooner would be better. Important foreign leaders were notified. Rusk met with Soviet ambassador Anatoly Dobrynin that afternoon to give him advance notice of Kennedy's speech. By all reports, Dobrynin left the meeting very shaken and upset. It is likely that the tight secrecy in Moscow that enveloped the operation didn't include him.

At seven o'clock that evening, the president went on television. Jet planes scrambled from bases in Florida and took up positions near Cuba to guard against any immediate retaliation.

Kennedy didn't try to sugarcoat or soft pedal the alarming news. "This Government, as promised, has maintained the closest surveillance of the Soviet military buildup on the island of Cuba," he began. "Within the past week, unmistakable evidence has established the fact that a series of offensive missile sites is now in preparation on that imprisoned island. The purpose of these bases can be none other than to provide a nuclear strike capability against the Western Hemisphere."[1]

He spoke about the danger that so many U.S. cities were facing. He outlined the steps that the United States would undertake: the quarantine, continued surveillance of Cuba, an emergency meeting of the United Nations Security Council, and additional measures. He closed by urging Khrushchev "to eliminate this clandestine, reckless and provocative threat to world peace and to stable relations between our two nations . . . to move the world back from the abyss of destruction."[2]

Some people in the capital believed that they would be incinerated that same night. "A reporter asked her husband whether they should head for the air-raid shelter nearest their home, at the Library of Congress," writes Kennedy biographer Ralph G. Martin. "They decided not to because they couldn't take their dog with them."[3]

All over the world, people realized that they were on the brink of nuclear war. They realized that the fate of the world literally depended on the decisions that two men—U.S. president John F. Kennedy and Soviet premier Nikita Khrushchev—would make in the next hours and days.

Soon dozens of U.S. Navy ships were in place. Their orders were simple. More than two dozen Soviet ships that seemed capable of carrying nuclear missiles were heading for Cuba. These vessels were to be halted and searched. If they refused to stop, the U.S. ships would open fire, aiming at the rudders of the Soviet ships to disable them.

The next day, October 23, was perhaps the most relaxed day during the crisis. The quarantine wouldn't officially take effect until the following morning. People in the nation's capital awoke and realized that war hadn't begun. Kennedy received some important diplomatic boosts. Two African nations refused to allow Soviet aircraft to land and refuel, which would be necessary if they were to fly to Cuba. The Organization of American States voted unanimously to support the quarantine. For ExComm, there was a personal benefit. Now that the news had been made public, the members could arrive openly. They began meeting regularly at the White House.

At first, Khrushchev was inclined to be belligerent. He ordered Soviet vessels to ignore the quarantine. He quickly withdrew that order, but he ordered construction on the missile sites to be speeded up.

In the meantime, so-called backdoor communications began to open up. Robert Kennedy met Ambassador Dobrynin at the Soviet Embassy. It was easier for the two men to talk in private rather than in the full glare of public scrutiny. Both men reported to their respective leaders. For Kennedy, it was easy. The White House was only a few minutes away. For Dobrynin, it was much more difficult. A messenger from the Western Union telegraph office would arrive on his bicycle to pick up the cables that Dobrynin wanted to send. Then the messenger would ride back to his office and send the cables to Moscow.

The blockade officially began at 10:00 A.M. on October 24. Two Soviet ships were within a few miles of the quarantine line. More ominously, a Soviet submarine was lurking nearby. U.S. government and military leaders became very tense.

Robert McNamara later described the ExComm meeting that began at the same time as one of the most anxious during the crisis. The U.S. aircraft carrier *Essex* and her escorts were heading toward the scene. They would order the submarine to come to the surface. If it didn't, it would be attacked. If that happened, the submarine would probably fight back.

Highly alert radar operators on board U.S. ships watched their screens. Soon they realized that the Soviet ships were slowing down. Then they stopped. By 10:25, a few of the ships had turned back. Not one tried to challenge the blockade.

At that point, Rusk said, "We're eyeball to eyeball and I think the other fellow just blinked."[4] This comment would become the most enduring phrase of the entire crisis.

Rusk had reason for his optimism. Tensions seemed to be easing, though the Soviets refused to acknowledge that they had accepted the terms of the quarantine. What no one in ExComm apparently realized was that the Soviets didn't want any of their equipment to fall into American hands, as it almost certainly would have if ships carrying it had tried to run the blockade.

The following day, October 25, naval ships allowed an oil tanker to proceed past the quarantine line because it was carrying non-military cargo necessary for the comfort of the Cuban people. On the same day, U.S. ambassador Adlai Stevenson addressed the United Nations. He demanded that Soviet ambassador Valerian Zorin answer the question of whether his country had installed offensive missiles.

Zorin replied, "In due course, sir, you will have your reply."

Stevenson's response became famous: "I am prepared to wait for my answer until Hell freezes over, if that is your decision."[5]

He further embarrassed Zorin by displaying some of the more incriminating U-2 photos. It was unusual to display top-secret intelligence materials, but it was considered important to prove that the missiles existed. Many nations still believed that the United States had been looking for an excuse to invade Cuba.

By then it had become apparent that the Soviets were respecting the quarantine. All the Soviet ships had turned back. That morning, October 25, the U.S. Navy had boarded a freighter that had been leased to the Soviets by Lebanon. It was a milder gesture than boarding a Soviet-owned ship. When it was clear that the vessel contained no offensive weapons, it was allowed to proceed.

On the other hand, it was apparent that the Soviets had accelerated the assembly process on land. Ever since Kennedy's speech, crews had been working around the clock preparing the missiles for readiness. Plans for the combined invasion and air strike moved into high gear. U.S. armed forces were ordered to DEFCON 2—the highest ever level of military readiness in peacetime and just one step short of war.

Then it began to appear that Khrushchev would give in. One indication was a somewhat bizarre meeting between John Scali, a correspondent with ABC-TV, and a Soviet agent named Alexander Fomin. Fomin expressed fear of war. He asked Scali to use his connections at the State Department to see if the United States would pledge not to invade Cuba. In return, Khrushchev would withdraw the missiles.

Three hours later, President Kennedy received a long letter from Khrushchev. The letter described the suffering that would result from a nuclear war and urged the president to show restraint. More important,

Khrushchev said that the crisis would end if Kennedy guaranteed not to invade Cuba.

ExComm assumed that the two developments were related. It is likely that the members went to bed that night feeling that the worst was over. They were wrong.

Relations turned ugly the following day. Khrushchev sent another letter. This time he demanded that the United States remove its missiles from Turkey. Kennedy was furious that Khrushchev had changed his mind again.

There was another problem. Comparing the two sets of missiles was like comparing apples and oranges. There weren't as many missiles in Turkey as there were in Cuba, they had been installed openly, and Turkey was not considered a trouble spot. Also, the United States already had plans to remove them. They would be replaced by much more secure—and powerful—Polaris missiles carried on American missile submarines that would be on constant patrol in the Mediterranean. The problem with Khrushchev's new demand was that no NATO member could put any faith in Kennedy's pledges of support if he appeared to cave in to Soviet pressure in this instance. ExComm went back to work on their air strike and invasion plans.

About noon, the members received another dose of bad news. The Cubans had shot down a U-2. The pilot, Rudolph Anderson, was dead.

Earlier in the week, ExComm had decided that if any U.S. planes were shot down, the SAM battery responsible would be taken out in an air strike.

The day became known as Black Saturday. It appeared that the shooting was about to start.

After finding out that the Soviet Union had acquired nuclear weapons, citizens of the United States realized that they could be the targets of attacks by Soviet aircraft and guided missiles. They would need some sort of civil defense.

In 1950, President Harry Truman created the Federal Civil Defense Administration (FCDA), which was somewhat similar to today's Homeland Security Department. While the FCDA instituted a number of programs, the two most famous were "duck and cover" classroom drills and the building of fallout shelters.

Many people still remember the monthly drills they went through at school. Their teachers would suddenly call out, "Drop!" They would quickly crawl under their desks, holding their arms over their heads. Sometimes classes on upper floors would hurry downstairs to the basement, which was considered a safer place in the event of a nuclear explosion.

Many of these youngsters had homes with fallout shelters in the backyard. The shelters ranged from what were little more than holes dug in the ground and covered with a couple of feet of dirt to elaborate multiroom facilities with beds, toilets, and supplies of food, water, and entertainment for lengthy stays.

WWII Ground Observer Corps

The Ground Observer Corps (GOC), which originated during World War II, was revived in 1950. It was designed to fill gaps between radar installations, with thousands of stations on the East and West Coasts and the Canadian border. These were constantly manned by volunteers with high-powered binoculars searching for low-flying Soviet bombers. To attract volunteers, the GOC ran ads such as "The Reds right now have about a thousand bombers that are quite capable of destroying at least 89 American cities in one raid. . . . Won't you help protect your country, your town, your children?"[6] The ads were effective: Nearly a million people signed up.

Fortunately, these programs were never needed. The Soviets never launched an attack. Soon after the Cuban missile crisis ended, the United States and the Soviet Union agreed to the Limited Test Ban Treaty. Under its terms, the two countries agreed not to test nuclear weapons in the atmosphere, in outer space, or under the ocean's surface. The world began to seem safer, and most people lost interest in civil defense.

A U.S. Jupiter guided missile at a site in Turkey. The first Jupiter missiles were delivered to the Air Force late in 1957.

The Jupiter missile had a range of nearly 2,000 miles. The "flower petal" structure at the base isn't part of the missile. It allows technicians to work on the missile if the weather is bad.

The Crisis Ends

U.S. military officials angrily demanded an air strike to take out the SAM site that had brought down Anderson. They ordered bombers to get ready. As soon as Kennedy gave the order, the planes would roar aloft. Some members of ExComm were also concerned that Khrushchev's second letter was an attempt to stall for time, because the Soviets were still working to get the missile sites ready.

There was a great deal of pressure on the president when ExComm met on Saturday afternoon. Yet Kennedy wanted to make one last effort to solve the crisis without military action.

At that point, Robert Kennedy came up with an idea. ExComm would react as if the second letter had never been received. The president would agree to the terms of the first letter: removal of the Soviet missiles in exchange for a pledge not to invade Cuba. Robert Kennedy went to see Dobrynin. After reassuring him that his brother did not want war, he became blunt: Agree to withdraw your missiles from Cuba within twenty-four hours or we will launch a massive air strike. At the same time, he held out a carrot. While there could be no public announcement, the Jupiter missiles would be quietly removed from Turkey within a few months. Dobrynin conveyed the terms to Khrushchev.

At precisely nine o'clock on the following morning, Khrushchev went on the radio to announce his decision.

He would accept Kennedy's pledge. The missiles would be withdrawn. There would be no nuclear war.

For the handful of men who had overseen the successful outcome, there would be the chance to resume a somewhat normal life. "Today I will be able to see my kids, for I have been entirely absent from home,"[1] said Robert Kennedy.

For his brother, the time that Robert and the other ExComm members had spent away from their homes had been well worth the sacrifice. President Kennedy was grateful for the extraordinary effort that they had put into their deliberations. He later said, "If we had had to act in the first twenty-four hours, I don't think . . . we would have chosen as prudently as we did."[2]

The president refused to be jubilant. He realized that it was important to allow Khrushchev to save face. The following day, congratulations to Kennedy poured in from around the country and around the world. No congratulations, however, came from Cuba. Castro was furious, both with the Soviets and with the Americans. Both sides had ignored him during the tense negotiations.

He wasn't the only one who was unhappy. The Cuban exiles in south Florida had looked forward to returning in the wake of an invasion that they were confident would have been successful. Though the Joint Chiefs of Staff accepted the president's decision, they too had hoped for a military victory.

The Soviets acted swiftly to keep their end of the bargain. By November 1, U-2 overflights indicated that several missile sites had been dismantled. The missiles were removed, taken back to Havana, and loaded onto Soviet cargo ships.

One stumbling block remained. The Soviets had also supplied the Cuban air force with a number of jet bombers. Castro insisted that they belonged to him, a gift from the Soviets. Kennedy insisted that the bombers had to go too. Finally Khrushchev persuaded Castro to release them.

On November 20, the United States lifted the naval quarantine. Soon afterward, the bombers were removed on Soviet ships. The ships' crews left part of the crates open so that aerial photographs would reveal that the bombers were inside. All forty-two were soon accounted for.

The following spring, Castro made a monthlong visit to the Soviet Union, where he received an especially warm welcome. At about the same time, the United States quietly removed its Jupiter missiles from Turkey. The two governments also negotiated an agreement that provided for a special telephone hotline between the two capitals. That way the leaders of the two superpowers could contact each other directly, rather than waiting hours or even days for letters and cables to go back and forth.

Both Kennedy and Khrushchev remained on the world stage for only a short time after the crisis ended. Kennedy was assassinated in Dallas, Texas, on November 22, 1963. While several official commissions have determined that the sniper, Lee Harvey Oswald, acted alone, to this day many people believe otherwise. Some believe that the Mafia might have been involved. Others insist that it was the work of anti-Castro Cubans who were upset because Kennedy agreed not to overthrow Castro.

In October 1964, Khrushchev was overthrown and replaced by Leonid Brezhnev, a cautious man who was careful not to overextend his country's power. Khrushchev lived in humble surroundings until his death seven years later.

Fidel Castro resisted all efforts to overthrow him. In January 2005, he celebrated the 46th anniversary of his accession to power. No world leader at that time had been in power longer than he had. He spanned the terms of eight more American presidents, as well as four Soviet premiers before the demise of the Soviet Union in 1991. Cuba remained one of the few openly Communist governments in the world.

FOR YOUR INFORMATION

The son of a coal miner, Nikita Khrushchev was born on April 17, 1894, in the Ukraine, which was part of Russia at that time. After a few years of school, he went to work as a pipefitter. He joined the Russian Communist Party during World War I and fought for the Communists in the civil war that broke out soon afterward.

When the war was over he became active in local party activities and steadily rose in importance. In 1938 he was named secretary of the Ukrainian Communist Party. The following year, he became a member of the Politburo, the party's central governing organization. With the outbreak of World War II, he was placed in charge of organizing resistance to the German army in the Ukraine.

Nikita Khrushchev

Within a few months after the death of Soviet dictator Joseph Stalin in 1953, Khrushchev won the power struggle within the party and became first secretary, the most important party position in the Soviet Union. He executed his main rival, Laventry Beria. Three years later, he began a program of de-Stalinization, which sought to downplay the importance of the former leader by accusing him of murdering millions of his countrymen. In 1958, Khrushchev became premier.

During his time in power, he tried to make life better for the people of the Soviet Union. He emphasized economic competition with the United States and other Western nations, rather than open hostility. He also boosted the Soviet Union's space program. Yet he was afraid that his country was falling further and further behind in the arms race with the United States; this prompted his decision to install offensive missiles in Cuba.

For years, many Communist officials had looked unfavorably upon some of Khrushchev's behavior. He had a reputation for acting foolishly on important international occasions, often interrupting speeches and yelling insults. Once he even took off one of his shoes and banged it on a table. Coupled with the perceived humiliation of the missile crisis, it was enough to cause his overthrow in 1964. He spent seven years under house arrest in Moscow before his death on September 11, 1971.

Chronology

(All dates 1962)

May 24	Soviet premier Nikita Khrushchev's plan to install offensive missiles in Cuba is approved by other Soviet leaders
Late July	First Soviet ships carrying missiles and other equipment arrive in Cuba
September 4	President John F. Kennedy publicly declares that installation of offensive weapons in Cuba is not acceptable
October 14	U.S. U-2 spy plane flies photographic reconnaissance mission over western Cuba
October 15	Photo analysts examining U-2 photos discover installation of offensive ballistic missiles
October 16	Kennedy learns of the existence of missiles; he convenes Executive Committee of the National Security Council (ExComm)
October 17	Kennedy travels to Connecticut for campaign trip; ExComm continues deliberations
October 18	Kennedy meets with Soviet foreign minister Andrei Gromyko
October 19	Kennedy leaves for campaign swing through the Midwest
October 20	Announcing that he has a "cold," Kennedy returns to Washington, D.C.; decides on blockade as the best solution to the crisis
October 21	Kennedy asks the *New York Times* and the *Washington Post* to withhold stories about Cuba
October 22	Kennedy announces a "quarantine" of Cuba during a nationally televised speech
October 23	Organization of American States supports the quarantine
October 24	Quarantine officially begins; Soviet ships turn around when they reach the quarantine line
October 25	U.S. ambassador Adlai Stevenson confronts Soviet ambassador Valerian Zorin in the United Nations
October 26	Khrushchev apparently agrees to withdraw missiles in exchange for U.S. pledge not to invade Cuba
October 27	Black Saturday: Khrushchev demands withdrawal of U.S. missiles from Turkey; U.S. spy plane is shot down over Cuba
October 28	Khrushchev announces decision to remove missiles
November 20	Kennedy lifts the quarantine

43

Timeline in History

1898   U.S. victory in Spanish-American War ends Spanish control over Cuba.

1902   Cuba becomes an independent nation.

1917   Communists come to power in Russia. John F. Kennedy is born.

1918   U.S. troops join soldiers from other nations in trying to help revolutionaries overthrow the new Communist government of Russia.

1922   The Soviet Union, consisting of Russia and three other republics, is formed; eventually eleven more republics are included.

1926   Fidel Castro is born.

1933   Fulgencio Batista becomes Cuban dictator.

1939   World War II begins with the German invasion of Poland.

1941   Germany invades the Soviet Union. Japan bombs Pearl Harbor and the United States enters the war.

1944   Batista retires.

1945   U.S. drops atomic bombs on Japanese cities of Hiroshima and Nagasaki; World War II ends.

1946   British Prime Minister Winston Churchill makes his famous "iron curtain" speech.

1948   The Berlin airlift begins when the Soviets block overland access; it ends eleven months later.

1949   Soviet Union conducts first successful test of an atomic bomb. The United States, Canada, and ten European countries form the North Atlantic Treaty Organization (NATO).

1952   Batista is returned to power in Cuba.

1953   Nikita Khrushchev becomes first secretary of the Communist Party following the death of Joseph Stalin.

1955   Eastern European nations sign the Warsaw Pact.

1957   Soviets launch *Sputnik I*, the first artificial earth satellite.

1958   Nikita Khrushchev becomes premier of the Soviet Union.

1959   Fidel Castro overthrows Batista and takes control of Cuba.

1960   Castro signs trade agreement with the Soviet Union. John F. Kennedy defeats Richard M. Nixon in U.S. presidential election.

1961   United States breaks off diplomatic relations with Cuba; Bay of Pigs invasion is a fiasco that greatly embarrasses Kennedy.

1962   The Cuban Missile Crisis puts the U.S. and Soviet Union face to face.

1963   The United States and the Soviet Union sign the Limited Test Ban Treaty. Telephone hotline provides direct connection between Washington, D.C., and Moscow. John F. Kennedy is assassinated.

1964   Khrushchev is removed from power. United States dramatically increases its involvement in the Vietnam War.

1971   Khrushchev dies.

1973   Batista dies.

1975   The last U.S. troops leave Vietnam.

1989   The Berlin Wall is dismantled.

1991   The Warsaw Pact is dissolved. The Soviet Union collapses.

2005   Fidel Castro begins his 46th year in power.

Chapter Notes

Chapter 1 The Roots of a Conflict

1. CNN Cold War—Historical Documents—"The Sinews of Peace"
   http://www.cnn.com/SPECIALS/cold.war/episodes/02/documents/churchill/

Chapter 2 Unmasking a Deception

1. Robert Weisbrot, *Maximum Danger: Kennedy, the Missiles, and the Crisis of American Confidence* (Chicago: Ivan R. Dee, 2001), p. 64.

Chapter 3 ExComm

1. Ralph G. Martin, *A Hero for Our Time: An Intimate Story of the Kennedy Years* (New York: Macmillan, 1983), p. 461.

Chapter 4 To the Brink

1. Aleksandr Fursenko and Timothy Naftali, *"One Hell of a Gamble": Khrushchev, Castro, and Kennedy 1958–1964* (New York: W. W. Norton & Company, 1997), pp. 245–46.

2. Ibid., p. 246.

3. Ralph G. Martin, *A Hero for Our Time: An Intimate Story of the Kennedy Years* (New York: Macmillan, 1983), p. 467.

4. Lawrence Freedman, *Kennedy's Wars: Berlin, Cuba, Laos and Vietnam* (New York: Oxford University Press, 2000), p. 197.

5. Adlai Stevenson and the Cuban Missile Crisis
   http://infoshare1.princeton.edu/libraries/firestone/rbsc/mudd/online_ex/stevenson_speech/

6. Ground Observer Corps
   http://www.radomes.org/museum/documents/GOC/GOC.html

Chapter 5 The Crisis Ends

1. Lawrence Freedman, *Kennedy's Wars: Berlin, Cuba, Laos and Vietnam* (New York: Oxford University Press, 2000), p. 217.

2. Robert Weisbrot, *Maximum Danger: Kennedy, the Missiles, and the Crisis of American Confidence* (Chicago: Ivan R. Dee, 2001), p. 122.

Glossary

arms race

A competition to see who can build up more and deadlier weapons.

ballistic missile

(buh-LISS-tick MISS-ul)—missile designed to attack targets over long distances; it is launched high into the air or space and follows a predetermined course.

charismatic

(khar-iz-MAH-tik)—Inspiring an especially high degree of loyalty or enthusiasm.

clandestine

(klan-DES-tun)—Secret.

exiles

(EK-siles)—People who are forced to leave their native country and live elsewhere.

fallout

Debris and radioactive particles that fall back to earth after a nuclear explosion.

foment

(FOE-ment)—To promote the development of.

hallucinogenic

(hah-loo-sih-neh-JEH-nik)—A substance that makes a person have visions of things that aren't real.

Joint Chiefs of Staff

Advisory committee consisting of the heads of the U.S. Army, Air Force, Navy, and Marine Corps.

missile

(MISS-ul)—anything that is thrown or propelled; can range from rocks and arrows to rockets with nuclear warheads.

Reds

Communists.

repugnant

(rih-PUG-nunt)—Contradictory, distasteful.

For Further Reading

For Young Adults

Brubaker, Paul. *The Cuban Missile Crisis in American History*. Berkeley Heights, NJ: Enslow Publishers, 2001.

Carter, E. J. *20th-Century Perspectives: The Cuban Missile Crisis*. Chicago: The Heinemann Library, 2003.

Chrisp, Peter. *The Cuban Missile Crisis*. Milwaukee, WI: World Almanac Library, 2002.

Finkelstein, Norman H. *Thirteen Days/Ninety Miles: The Cuban Missile Crisis*. New York: Julian Messner/Simon & Schuster, 1994.

Gow, Catherine Hester. *The Cuban Missile Crisis*. San Diego: Lucent Books, 1997.

McConnell, William S. *Living Through the Cuban Missile Crisis*. San Diego: Greenhaven Books, 2005.

Works Consulted

Freedman, Lawrence. *Kennedy's Wars: Berlin, Cuba, Laos and Vietnam*. New York: Oxford University Press, 2000.

Fursenko, Aleksandr, and Timothy Naftali. *"One Hell of a Gamble": Khrushchev, Castro, and Kennedy 1958–1964*. New York: W. W. Norton & Company, 1997.

Huchthausen, Peter A. *October Fury*. Hoboken, NJ: Peter Wiley & Sons, 2002.

Martin, Ralph G. *A Hero for Our Time: An Intimate Story of the Kennedy Years*. New York: Macmillan, 1983.

Weisbrot, Robert. *Maximum Danger: Kennedy, the Missiles, and the Crisis of American Confidence*. Chicago: Ivan R. Dee, 2001.

On the Internet

Cuban Missile Crisis
http://www.cubanmissilecrisis.org/

The Cuban Missile Crisis, 1962: A Political Perspective After 40 Years
http://www2.gwu.edu/~nsarchiv/nsa/cuba_mis_cri/

The Cuban Missile Crisis, October 18–29, 1962
http://www.hpol.org/jfk/cuban/

Adlai Stevenson and the Cuban Missile Crisis
http://infoshare1.princeton.edu/libraries/firestone/rbsc/mudd/online_ex/stevenson_speech/

The Atomic Spy Ring
http://www.cnn.com/SPECIALS/cold.war/experience/spies/spy.files/infiltration/spyring.html

CNN Cold War—Historical Documents—"The Sinews of Peace"
http://www.cnn.com/SPECIALS/cold.war/episodes/02/documents/churchill/

Fourteen Days in October: The Cuban Missile Crisis
http://www.thinkquest.org/library/site_sum.html?tname=11046&url=11046/

Greenberg, David. "Fallout Can Be Fun."
http://slate.msn.com/id/2078892/

Ground Observer Corps
http://www.radomes.org/museum/documents/GOC/GOC.html

Nikita Khrushchev
http://www.spartacus.schoolnet.co.uk/RUSkhrushchev.htm

President Kennedy and the Cuban Missile Crisis
http://www.learningcurve.gov.uk/heroesvillains/jfk/default.htm

Index